CW00547574

ETTRICK & ELSEWHERE

Selected Poems

by

Judy Steel

Illustrations by Cath Rutherford

Cover design by Iain Black

For the Aikwood Steels –
Rory, Vicki, Eilidh and Duggie.

For David, as always.

In memory of James Rutherford (1952-2023)
Master Printer

INTRODUCTION

When I was a little girl, somebody asked me the question, "What do you want to be when you grow up?" to which I replied, "I want to be a farmer's fat wife and write poetry in my spare time". Well, I am now indubitably fat, although (thank goodness) I married a politician and not a farmer. Subsequent early career choices that appealed to me were to be Scotland's first Prime Minister and/or the first woman to stand at the South Pole. (I had a necrophiliac crush on Captain Scott of the Antarctic, while the agricultural ambition was the result of an idyllic farm holiday at the age of six.)

But politics and poetry have continued to be passions since my mid-teens. Even my first published poem was a political diatribe against the Russian invasion of Hungary in 1956. My oevre is not substantial, but I hope the poems communicate the sights and sounds and emotions that inspired them, and give enjoyment to you, their readers.

Judy Steel
Selkirk 2023

ACKNOWLEDGEMENTS

Several of the poems have been published previously by *Lines Review, Chapman, The Herald, the Eildon Tree, The New Minstrelsy of the Scottish Border,* and *Scotland's Poetry.*

The cover was designed by Iain Black, the book's layout and illustrations by Cath Rutherford and the printing by Richardson and Son Printers, Hawick. Gerda Stevenson not only contributed the foreword but also did a painstaking job on editing and early proof-reading. My daughter Catriona was also a crucial outside eye in these last tasks.

To all of these I give my grateful thanks.

ETTRICK & ELSEWHERE
by Judy Steel

First published in 2023
Copyright © Judy Steel, November 2023

ISBN No. 9781916980013

All rights reserved. No part of this publication may be reproduced, stored in a retrieval system, or transmitted in any form or by any means, electronic or mechanical, including photocopying and recording, without prior permission in writing from the copyright holder.

FOREWORD

Judy Steel is deeply rooted in her beloved Scottish Borders, and so it's not surprising that her poetry is too. She writes about the things she cherishes – family, community and place. For Judy, landscape and buildings potently resonate with the past as if she's living side by side with people long gone, treading in their invisible footprints. Her poems about lovingly restoring ancient Aikwood Tower, her home for two decades, pay moving homage to those who came before her: stone masons, craftsmen and residents. Continuity is her constant theme – the past always connecting with the energy of the present.

Local culture, in all its colour, is vividly brought to life in these pages, and often in the voice of its people – Judy writes with a love of the Borderers' Scots language, lyrical, earthy and tender by turn. In her extended poem, *Hawick Common Riding,* she creates a vibrant portrait of the famous community festival of the same name, conjuring the excitement of the horsemanship, and the cast of rich characters involved.

Many of these poems are tributes to friends and family, none more touching than *The Ballad of the Thistle and the Lotus,* an epithalamium written for her daughter and Indian son-in-law.

A woman who enjoys travel, Steel takes us to France, Scandinavia, India, Africa and the Caribbean, and shares her relish for other cultures.

She also reveals a refreshingly feisty lack of decorum in her hilarious narrative poem *Rab's Midnight Fart.*

The final sequence expresses her admiration for the Border ballads. Inspired by them, she has too, written her own songs in ballad form. And very singable they are too. Some have already been set to music, having been part of Selkirk's Rowan Tree Theatre, the company which Steel herself established and spearheaded for nearly thirty years.

Her love of the beautiful Ettrick valley, its history and people, courses though her stanzas. I've no doubt that the fervour of her rootedness will speak not only to those native to that part of the world, but to many from elsewhere.

Gerda Stevenson, 2023.

CONTENTS

Prologue   *page*

Lunch at Tibbie's   7

Part One: Ettrick

The Solstice Stone   9
Benign Invasion   10
Awakening   11
Windows   12
Deshabillement   12
Restoration Job   13
First Night   14
January Dance   15
Silver and Gold   16
The Hedgehog's Funeral   17
The Auld Hoose   21

Part Two: Elsewhere

Lauder Common Riding   23
Pan Am 103   24
Bield   25
Huntlyburn Haiku   25
Rab's Midnight Fart   26
Hawick Common Riding   27
Driving to My Daughter's House   30
Le Cathedral des Vins   31
Memory Lane   32
Videy Island, Reykavik   32
Freetown   33
Monks Risborough   34

contd. over

CONTENTS *continued*

Holi at Udaipur   36
Butterfly Girls   37
Shoelaces   38
Carribean Morning   40
Gullfoss   41
Three in the Marriage   42

Part Three – Songs, ballads and opera

The Plain Girl's Lament   45
Birdsong   46
Bride's Song   47
The Ballad of the Thistle and the Lotus   48
Song of a Long-Ago Ride   50
Timbuktu 72 days   51
The March Riders' Song   52
The Ballad of Auld Norman's Party   54

Epilogue

Life is aPerilous Voyage   58

Appendix: Music Scores

The Plain Girl's Lament   59
Birdsong   60
Bride's Song   61
The Ballad of the Thistle and the Lotus   62
Timbukto 76 Days   64
The March Riders' Song   66

Glossary   68

Prologue

LUNCH AT TIBBIE'S

In memory of James Hogg

From a sepia print
nonagenarian Tibbie Shiel
iron jawed beneath moustache and goffered bonnet
surveys through stern and rheumy eyes
her twentieth century guests:

walkers with wind-fresh hair, Icelandic sweaters
swinging their healthy way from coast to coast;
brash, bright anoraked camera crews
invading the calm contentment of the day.
Above, jet airplanes scream through cloudless blue
and splinter St. Mary's loch's autumnal peace -
foretellers, not phantoms, of a violent doom.

Ah well –
no day is quite perfect.
But outside
black spotted sycamore leaves drift down,
ready to scrunch beneath unhurried feet,
and the Ettrick Shepherd awaits our homage.

Meantime, Tibbie watches us
devouring thick barley soup, moist doughnuts,
and fat-fleshed Yarrow trout
from the fish farm.

In 1985, I ran a three-week long festival commemorating 150 years since the death of James Hogg, "The Ettrick Shepherd", poet, novelist, journalist and short story writer. I knew nothing about running festivals, and not much about James Hogg, but what I lacked in knowledge I made up for in enthusiasm and imagination.

PART ONE
Ettrick

THE SOLSTICE STONE

For Rory

Dismembering the Eden of dead apple trees
on midsummer's day
I uncovered a sunburst of stone
amongst the swineweed fronds.
What mason's hands, with gnarls and scars
to match the apple's bark
gouged out with careful chisel
these worn radials?
What Aikwood laird instructed him
in the embellishment of a new-born tower?

In the midge-laden dusk
my mind creates the donors
of my solstice gift.

*In 1989 David, my
husband, and I
began the renovation
of Aikwood, a 16th
century Border
Tower near Selkirk.
For the first year,
all was paperwork
and we couldn't
touch the fabric of
the building. The
garden was another
matter. Once a
fruitful kitchen
garden, it had been
used in later years
as a bullrun, which
meant it was a fertile
ground for weeds.*

*I wrote about
a dozen poems
during the two-year
restoration process.
This was the first.*

BENIGN INVASION

It's a russet day:
air hangs between damp and beaded mist.
A pheasant whirrs from tangled branches
and the tower is ripe with her mysteries.

The oak door swings inwards.
Rubber soled invaders
run up the Kerry-handed stairs;
unhardened fingers caress old crevices,
trace the names in crumbled lime
of lover, farmhand, prisoner of war.

Old chaff lies sterile on the pitted flags,
a legacy of harvests reaped and threshed
by long-dead holders of the pencilled names.
Now other seeds germinate,
and in her many-chambered womb
the tower feeds the embryos of imagination.

Such a day casts no shadow.
Tower-captivated, the invaders sit
cross-legged on cobbles, bielded by grey walls,
telling new tales of old and unknown times.
They mark the present out beside the past
and leave new names scratched on the plaster page.

The youth theatre director John Haswell and I started the Borders Youth Theatre as a project within the 2nd Borders Festival of Ballads and Legends, in 1989. One afternoon, we brought a group of young people to Aikwood.

AWAKENING

For Graeme and Lynne

Above the golden tubes of harvest straw,
above the black ridges of the steading roofs,
above the eternal curves of Ettrick's hills
twilight surrenders to moonlight
and a full fat moon for hallow's eve
splashes through the re-opened embrasure,
and spills on the firestone floor.

The place lies quiet: no ghost stirs
awakened by the disturbance of old walls;
there's no infernal echo of a wizard's call;
but the moon must find it magical
that after two thousand obstructed revolutions
she finds her old accustomed place
on the flags of Aikwood's hall.

*My son Graeme
and his partner
Lynne worked
enthusiastically on
the restoration of
Aikwood and a few
years later, they were
married in the Great
Hall by Graeme's
grandfather.*

11

WINDOWS

For Falconer and Russell Grieve

O, you have made me magic windows
that open – not on foam,
but on enchanted forests
where red squirrels make their home.

They open on the treetops,
and align me with the birds,
you made me gates to fairy lands,
all I can return are words.

DESHABILLEMENT

In memory of Dave Bunyan, master mason

In the April sunshine
they uncorset the tower –
men from the west with urban oaths
that fall strangely on the valley air.

Removed from her chrysalis of scaffolding,
she stands, sun-roseate and vibrant,
as though the Selkirk masons' hands
had been Pygmalion, the sculptor-king's,
carving life through charmed chisel
into receptive stone.

The city men depart,
leaving detritus of crisps and Irn-Bru,
and Aikwood, resplendent in her nakedness
returns to the caresses
of her small-town lovers.

All the external work – roofing, sarking, leadworks, laying of rafters and flooring, was carried out over the winter of 1990-91. Dave Bunyan and his son Andrew were the principal masons; they were also superb ex-Army pipers, and sometimes in the lunch hour would practice in the Great Hall.

RESTORATION JOB

Cadaver-like, its extremities green-moulded,
the oak door lies on trestles in the shed.
Above its surface, scarred by unknown weapons,
Andrew plies resuscitating tools.

The door is ancient, massy, crudely hewn:
dovetails and dowels sit strangely in it now;
in all the centuries no hands have smoothed it,
no touch, no skills as fine-tuned as today's.

There's a quality to men who work with timber
that recall to me the best of childhood's years,
when I learned to tell of grains, and bark, and buddings,
from one whose span was spent with living trees.

As fine shavings spiral out from Andrew's planing,
and fine sawdust floats from underneath his hands,
the sights and scents of distant days are near me,
and stilled voices sound approval in my ears.

Perhaps, if I continue to be fortunate,
such kindly hands will kist me when it's time:
round out that final O of life's last journey
and prepare me for the dust from which I came.

Then my flesh-freed ghost may hear known voices talking -
but not, please God, in mournful undertones -
of the day the Saltire flew again at Aikwood
and the night we sang and feasted in her hall.

*Towards the finish
of the restoration
we held an open
day for the press,
and a feast at night
for all the men who
worked on it. It was
a magnificent night,
with the sealing up
of a time capsule,
whole legs of roast
lamb, lashings of
wine and singing
of local songs.
It was the 1st of
many celebrations
at Aikwood.*

FIRST NIGHT

I slept at the tower last night –
a stolen night, unauthorised, alone –
and, much to my surprise, I never thought:
who slept here last?
The widowed farmer with his flowing beard?
The one-legged tramp befriended by his son?

I never wondered who, of my own gender,
cocooned in comfort under soft white quilt,
last saw the morning lighten through the dormer
and heard the mavis carol in the dawn.

I sensed no tremors out of Aikwood's history:
no ghosts of Roman soldiers spied on me;
I heard no reiver's horse disturb the forest,
no sound of mirth or quarrel in the hall.

Which is the jingler's room that legend tells of?
Where is the wizard turning lead to gold?
All is benign: beneath the curving plaster
the walls breathe kindliness and great goodwill;
for there's been magic practiced here, by alchemists
of sturdy frame and steady hand and eye,
innerly grace and soft-toned Border voices
who've stemmed decay, turned ruin into home.
These are the presences in door, on stairway,
who lay to rest all dangers from past times.

I spent my first night (and my last, twenty years later) at Aikwood not in the master bedroom with its impressive fireplace and its half-tester bed, but in the smallest and cosiest of the four bedrooms: "The Blue Room".

JANUARY DANCE

For Janice (Chic) Parker

In the small glen the naked larch trees dance –
their russet bodies in the lowering light
choreographed by January's gales
and bounded by the earthing of old roots.

Framed by my kitchen window
two slender ash trees lead the larches' chorus
in a sylvan pas-de-deux,
while far upstage
where wild glen marches with tame pasture
the aged pines of Caledonia move robustly
in totally clothed decency.

When the blue-grey sky grows dark
there will be other dances:
of clouds that drift across the moon's broad face,
of flames that writhe round limbs of fallen trees.

Tomorrow all these dances will be done;
all frenzies quite outworn,
while from my kitchen sink
I'll watch the trees in their accustomed stillness
and their unclothedness will mourn
the free abandonment of dance.

Ah, well – it's not for long.
The snowdrops are exploding through tired winter turf,
and in a few more weeks
the larches will shimmer in the green haze
of spring's covenanted underwear.
And should they dare to dance,
their movements will be tempered
to a sedater measure
dictated by the quiet summer breeze.

SILVER AND GOLD

Silver. The horse was called Silver.
At over sixteen hands he stood:
kind-eyed, deep-chested, and with arching neck.
Such mounts are carved in stone or cast in bronze,
with kings or generals astride their backs
at vantage points in cities and big towns;
or on huge canvases, in painter's oils,
they prance as messengers from long-fled years.

But here, in this small town,
such times have substance still;
they ring, not echo in a present chime.
Men utter words fast losing currency
like honour, duty, pride and constancy,
and with these virtues bear the flag aloft.

Silver, the horse was called,
and answered to his name.
But on midsummer's smiling Friday morn,
the horses, hills, and all our memories
are deepest-veined, not tipped, with glowing gold.

THE HEDGEHOG'S FUNERAL

For Graeme and Catriona

In a hiatus that too often occurs
at summer Pony Club events
my children found a hedgehog.
It was young and full of fleas and floppy –
a peely-wally prickled pet.
In triumph, they brought it home and as an honour,
deposited it on the lap of an urban house guest
whose discomfort was far more pronounced
than his appreciation of their tribute.

There was a field beside our house
whose other march was Ettrick Water.
A small haugh lay between
where we kept the ponies.

The tenant farmer had loaned the ground that year
as a campsite for kids from Wester Hailes –
that deprived housing scheme on the fringes
of the Athens of the North.

Some of the villagers complained
that these children knew no boundaries;
that they stole flowers from gardens, tomatoes from greenhouses,
and didn't come to church.
>   *No like the Scout campers at aa. Nae manners.*
>   *They social workers need tae keep a better haud o them.*

contd. over

17

Even my placid husband uttered warningly:

When Armageddon comes, they'll remember.
They'll remember this village and its fecund gardens.

My under-tens made friends with the townies
and returned from the camp in awe:

They'd never seen hens!!
They don't know eggs come from hens!!
They've never seen cows!!
They don't know milk comes from cows!!

Urban and rural met in mutual wonder
at the alien nature of each others' lives,
but formed the fleeting bond of children anywhere.

Of course the pleasure of the little hedgehog was to be shared.
They set off for the camp; came home for tea,
And tucked their treasure in its box of hay.

> They'd never heard of hedgehogs!
> Their mums had never read them Mrs. Tiggywinkle!
> They wouldn't hold it! Not even the big boys!

The hedgehog seemed very sick and frail
and never even rolled into a ball.
Next morning it was dead. They didn't weep,
but organised its burial.

Along the road between the village school
and parish kirk,
the funerals of old folk that they knew
pass by the plate glass windows.
Children whisper eulogies:

> That's Mrs. Elliot's coffin. She died on Friday.
> She used to give us toffees.

The transient pleasure that the hedgehog brought
deserved an obsequy.
They fashioned a coffin from a shoebox,
veneered it with sky-blue wallpaper,
inserted carrying poles of bamboo cane
and placed a small posy on the lid.

contd. over

They marched across the haugh
and invited their new friends
to join the social occasion.

No-one came.
Death was a bogie to that streetwise gang,
not part of Nature's cycle.
Undismayed, my children bore the prickly corpse
to their redundant sandpit
and its somewhat shallow grave.
They executed the interment, said a prayer,
And returned to the kitchen
for a drink of juice.

THE AULD HOOSE

I have said goodbye,
walked through each stripped room
that once held our furniture
and the cornucopia of rubbish
acquired by growing families.
Now the walls are chilled, damp-patched;
here and there plaster crumbles,
paint flakes, an astragal rots:
the house waits for others to revive it.

In attics festooned with the small hard beads
of mice droppings, and thick grey dust,
I've uncovered baby clothes,
Sasha dolls, bagfuls of rosettes
and a pile of brittle records.

I've walked through the field, its hill and its haugh
trodden by the hooves of long-sold ponies;
made quiet reverence at the grave
of our kind black cob.

I've watched the Ettrick churn brown and high,
obliterating the shallows that we swam in,
whirling past the rocks we dived off,
spilling over camp and camp-fire sites,
and I remember when it froze enough
to bear foolhardy skaters.

We spent twenty-six happy years at Cherrydene. It was the first house we bought, and was where we brought up our children. They were dismayed at the thought of leaving it and the house retains a prime place in all our affections.

contd. over

I have re-lived all erratic judgements
made within these walls,
and peered regretfully down lanes
where wisdom, not wilfulness, might have been my guide.
Those ways are closed to me now,
like the door my keys have locked for the last time.

I have said goodbye: I will not
be like Lot's wife.

PART TWO

Elsewhere

LAUDER COMMON RIDING

For Lynne and Hannah.

Up on the once-contested moor
twelve hundred iron shoes
bruise the heather
and in the dry air
the scent of bell and ling
ascends to our lungs
mixed with the comforting scent
of hard-ridden horses.

In velvet hats and tie-pinned stocks,
hairnets and stretch breeches,
we bear scant similarity
to the riders we follow
across the centuries.

But –
lopsided in his saddle
on his grandfather's lead rein
a six-year old veteran
trots up the heathery hill.
"See that stane dyke?"
The auld yin says,
"That's the mairch.
That's why we hae the Common Riding."

Lauder Common Riding was the first Border Common Riding I rode at – in 1964. It was also the last, in 2014. In 2001 I won the cup for the oldest rider – the only cup I have ever won for riding or anything else. My saddle companion was often my daughter in law, Lynne. Now she and her daughter Hannah ride the Lauder marches together

RAB'S MIDNIGHT FART

THAT was the most impressive fart I've heard or smelt!
Never has any matched its power
since the lower maths class of 1956.

The teacher raised her desk-lid.
Then -
           Rumble! Rift! Fart!
An innocent voice (O horror! Mine!)
is heard piping flute-like:
             WHO did that?
Shock. Silence. More silence.
Suspension beckons, maybe expulsion.
More silence.
At last the unprecedented event:
The teacher *apologises.*

Fifty years later
Five decades later
Half a century later
I learned the truth:
That her desk was crammed with gin-bottles:
Full, half full, half empty, dry:
What fuel for a fart!

But yours, Rab, surpasses it fourfold. Congratulations!
Pardon me if I don't stay around to celebrate:
The corridor might detonate.

HAWICK COMMON RIDING = MEN

Though nowadays they let the weemin ride,
Hawick Common Riding still equals men.

Men, men:
at seevin in the mornin'
furst Friday efter furst Monday o' June –
men, booted, tight-breeched and bare heided
linger ootside High Street pubs,
near empty the ATMs,
heid for their horses.

Men, men:
baldy-heided men wi' paunches,
troosered in chinos, jeans or battered cords.
Atween the troosers and the baldy heids
they sport stripey shirts, and ties that boast
that yince they too threw booted legs ower the saiddle
and rade the lang weys through the mosses.

Men, men:
man and callant, in their saiddles,
the furst o' the day!
Faither and laddie, riding lang-reined and languidly,
they raise a cheer frae those on fit,
raise a cheer for the furst o' the day.

Men, men:
men on horses
come in their dizzens noo,
their cuddies smertened for this day o' days.

This is written with great affection for this notoriously male event, now inclusive of women as well. There was always an aura of testerone to Hawick Common Riding that took one back to reiving times. But once the rideouts were open to women, I was one of a few who, in 2000, followed the Cornet on his most challenging ride-out – to Mosspaul on the Dumfriesshire border - in 2000

contd. over

Manes are plaited,
tails a shimmerin waterfaa o hair,
coats glintin in the morning sun.
Clean-legged or shaggy-fetlocked,
ribbed-kisted, deep-barrelled, or thoroughbred-lean,
buckin or behavin, snortin or stallin –
aa revellin in the comfort o the herd.

Men, men:
men in green jaikets,
saxhorns in their haunds.
Men in coats o' blue an' gowd,
twigs o' aik in their bunnets,
fifes and flutes in their fingers,
drums on their hips,
aa at the ready for the first melodic blaw.

Men, men:
men wi faces
carved frae the land, the mills, the rugby fields –
yin or twae are wearin
the unmistakeable features o' the landit gentry,
matched by Panama hats, tweed jaikets, crested blazers,
hatbands and ties o' auld regiments
or far-off boardin schules.

Men, men:
men's voices singin the auld sang
that tells o a battle even aulder
an repeats that phrase sae ancient that
it's lost in the mirk o unrecorded history:
Teribus an Teriodin!

Men. Men:
men on horses, through Drumlanrig's airch!
There he leads them, king o' the day:
the Cornet, the Hawick Cornet!
Ahint him, Richt and Left Haund Men
an' Actin Faither.
And then, in yae streekit line
five hunnert horses.

Men, men:
mair an' mair men on horses:
auld-farrant seats (feet forrit,
bums weel back);
or cramped and curled up in the saiddle
in the jockey style the callants love to preen.
Ex-Cornets, future Cornets, would-be Cornets,
men frae ither touns,
auld men on steady mounts,
bairns on faithers' lead-reins,
an a' the hunnerts in between
follow their leader on this shining day.
Five hunnert years o history an horses
pass joyously the cheerfu, cheerin crowds.

Hawick Common Riding equals men;
but more nor that:
it maks a' men equal,
save fur the Cornet.

DRIVING TO MY DAUGHTER'S HOUSE

In the sluiced-out countryside
surplus water glistens;
rivulets run through lines of barley stubble
and the glaury troughs
of unharrowed furrows.

Droplets spray from rolling wheels
marking the riverside road;
detritus-shrouded trees emerge
marking the *medium filum*
of Tweed's familiar course.
Knee high in the current
stand sturdy elms and oaks,
waist-deep the willows;
while hazels, brambles, hawthorn stems
lie drowned entirely.

*The road from
Peebles to Selkirk
runs for several miles
beside the Tweed. On
a dark night, a full
moon will reflect in
the river; in daytime,
the various moods
and levels of it give
an ever-changing
picture.*

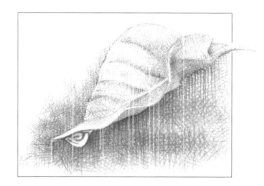

LE CATHEDRAL DES VINS, SAUMUR

For David and Daphne Pratt

1011 The monks burrowed these depths –
hewed out the stones, hauled them through broken fingernails,
torn tendons, shattered limbs and torsos,
(and broken, torn and shattered spirits too),
and with such human sacrifice they raised
a place of prayer to God.

1790 Revolution burns: its flames lick and gobble
not only tyrants in their palaces,
but the small people and the holy men,
the sound of quiet in the ancient cloisters.
Nothing remains between the earth and air
to mark the faith and peace of all those years.

2005 In the vaulted caves,
row on row and stack on stack
of green glass bottles testify
to how the monastic quarries now yield profit
for the vintners' trade.
Imprisoned bubbles lie ready to erupt
for weddings, births, and triumphs still unknown;
accountants' columns swell like ripening grapes,
and the vaults shout in joyful recollection
stone psalms to God and Bacchus side by side.

In the 1990s and 2000s we took part in a series of classic car rallies in Europe under the name "Claret and Classics". There was more laughter than competitiveness, and we saw many places that were off the main tourist route. David and Daphne Pratt have shared many of these somewhat daft times with us.

*I had my own pony
in my teens: a sturdy
Highlander called
Rosie. I was one of
only four young people
in Dunblane who
possessed ponies, and
none of us had the
use of a trailer. These
days, three of my
granddaughters own
six horses between them
and one, Persia, has
an HGV licence. They
hunt, compete, and
participate in the Border
Common Ridings.*

MEMORY LANE

I travelled this way decades ago:
a fat girl on a shaggy garron
trotting towards another gymkhana defeat.
The rain blurred my spectacles,
and the saddle squelched beneath my wet backside,
but the sodden reins slipping through my fingers
reeled out on paradise.

VIDEY ISLAND, REYKAVIK

Shadows stretch their silhouettes
against the midnight sun;
and old Joanna lies at last
happed in a blanket of cloud-coloured pansies
and the crisp white marble sheet
of the bed she sought langsyne.
And so the shades of Magnus and little Bjorne
return to the embrace
six decades awaiting them here.

How did you mark time, Joanna,
for those long, shorn years?
Who planted the pansies,
strewed today's fresh flowers,
and commissioned the sun-gilded testament
to your re-union?

FREETOWN

In memory of my mother, Ann MacGregor

Look down
on the tall tropical trees
from the hill,
as from o'er the descending layers
the poor look down on the puppet players,
and gaze at the palm-fringed shore
where the white surf breaks with unheard roar
on the golden sand;
and see the pale unruffled sea
rise to the sky like a wall
twixt us and the world of home.
And there lie ships
like us, imprisoned without the wall of sea,
lie, still at anchor in the shimmering heat,
waiting their chance to climb
to the other side, and meet
their freedom.

This is a cheat. When I started this project I was (and still am) also engaged on the never-ending task of clearing out family files and boxes. I found this on a scrap of paper in my mother's handwriting. I think it is hers and that it was written at some time between 1945 and 1947, when she and my father lived in Sierra Leone, leaving their four daughters in Scotland.

MONKS RISBOROUGH

For Mary Douglas-Bate (née Groves)

When I was ten my mother said:
There are new folk along the road
with a girl your age.

And I, greedy for friendship,
pedalled my bicycle along the street
of picture postcard cottages
and awaited your arrival –
an advent urchin in an Aertex shirt.

There followed two years' holidays
Teeming with the equine passions
of pre-pubertal girls.
Most of all, I remember
riding, barelegged and bridle-less
The old Welsh cob;
playing at circuses with
your rocking horse,
the contents of my dressing up chest,
and untrammelled imaginations;
listening on the radio to the Grand National
the year it was won by a mare called Nickel Coin;
lessons on lead reins around leafy Chiltern lanes,
and building foot-high jumping courses
for your patient golden Labrador.

I remember too that one wet afternoon
we decided to swear blood-sisterhood,
but quailed at the incision of the knife.

I spent three years in the south of England, never totally at home there and pining for Scotland. But the friendship I had with Mary Groves was the deepest of my childhood and one which lasted for long years.

Not that it mattered:
friendship endures with lesser rituals.
Near sixty years ago our paths diverged
and each re-union's served for a decade.
Still, at the close of each succeeding year
your sprawling writing on the envelope
reaches past children, husbands, present lives
and re-affirms the memories of those times.

HOLI AT UDAIPUR

They cast the colours here as well:
not as we do –
not flags, but clouds and jets
of powdered pigments matching nature's shades
beneath wide-grinning winter skies
in Rajasthan.

Bougeanvilla-bright and citrus-sharp,
pyramids of paint on market stalls
have stood in week-long readiness
for Holi's midnight fires and clamorous dawn.

Now, these colours are cast,
anointing necks and foreheads, arms and cheeks,
staining second-best saris and demoted dhotis.
Noon slides to post-meridian
and multicoloured souvenirs
are scrubbed from bodies, hair and clothes
on the segregated steps of bathing places
beside Lake Udaipur.

The town drowses in familiar fashion
and ganja-replete revellers start to count the days
till next year's Holi.

BUTTERFLY GIRLS

For India, Caledonia and Persia Bhatia

After the daytime's hot and hard-glazed glitter
the light fades fast. Against the darkening skies.
Across red sand with wings outstretched they flitter,
a trinity of jewel-bright butterflies.

Flower-harvest here comes in the gaudiest hues:
marigold oranges, bougainvillea pinks
rivalling the peacock's breast of gilded blues –
and silks of such now form their quivering wings.

Next week, six hands, tattooed with lines and swirls
by mehdi-wallahs in rich russet brown
will spread and stretch by reminiscing girls
to schoolmates in a grey-green Scottish town.

SHOELACES

For my sisters, Joan Duff and Fay Black

When we were tender, pudgy little bairns
Our mothers squeezed hard pebbly buttons
Through the gaps in the straps of our indoor shoes.
They buckled on Clark's sandals in summertime,
And they tied the laces of our Startrite shoes
With double bows when autumn came around.

In time, we learned to tie the bows ourselves.
Looping the laces with our small digits
Was a skill that we learned very early.
"She can tie her own shoelaces!"
Was the parental boast of Mums and Dads.

We were given cards with holes and coloured laces
To practice. Our loose and floppy efforts
often came undone.
We'd try again – and again –
And the hard-won achievement of the shoelace bow
Was a wee personal triumph,
A passport admitting us through
The first of the many barriers
To independence, adulthood.

Nowadays, shoes for toddlers' feet
Close with a pad of Velcro.
You can't miss. The hours spent
mastering the vagaries of shoelaces
no longer have their place in pre-school years.

Mothers' voices, warm with pride
No longer cry, *well done! You are a clever girl!*
And close their reassuring hands
Over our soft and skeely fists.

They miss all that, our grandchildren,
With their easy-fastening canvas trainers
And sparkly party slippers,
Firm on their feet with one confident stab.

Velcro's the answer for grandparents too,
As the old primary skills desert us.
Our septuagenarian fingers,
Age-mottled, arthritis-distorted,
Our backs, too stiff to bend,
Fail us at the challenge of tying laces.
And so our dragging feet
Take their steps towards the final barrier
Shod in shoes with Velcro's sticky pads.

CARRIBEAN MORNING

White mares' manes and tails
curl back on Caribbean waves,
spend themselves on golden sands.

Nearby, the island's thoroughfare
rumbles and thunders with early traffic:
workers stirred from sleep
move towards another day's toil.

But I'm vacationing.
I step between the elements:
no indrawn breath checks me;
no gooseflesh pimples rise
on my winter-white marbled skin.
The atmosphere's constant, and tropical
in solid sand, in liquid sea, in sun-warmed air.

GULLFOSS

For Rolf Jelnes

She was called Gullfoss
after the Icelandic waterfall
and she plied her passengers
from Reykavik to Leith,
then ploughed her furrow
across the North Sea -
up the Kattegat,
down the Skagerak,
past Hamlet's haunted Elsinore
where a bell tolled her passage.

She nudges her way
towards Copenhagen's heart:
curlicued spires rear up from red brick walls
clad in verdigrised copper.

The Gullfoss comes to rest
on the quayside.
A small boy hops on the spot,
in his hand my welcome gift,
a crumpled paper bag that traps
my first taste of Denmark:
a custard-filled sweet pastry: *Wienebrød*

I have arrived.
Wonderful, wonderful Copenhagen!

THREE IN THE MARRIAGE

For David, on our fifty-ninth wedding anniversary.

There were always three in our marriage –
you, Africa and me.
She was always your first love, Kenya:
a teenage passion that never faded
despite your proud Scottishness and despite
the separation of over fifteen years.

With love and pride you took me
to meet her when it was first possible.
I felt admiration, and respect, even affection
though passion was withheld.

———

We marvelled at the variegated game,
splashed in the Indian ocean with myriad crabs,
took the night train from coast to capital
and made new friends.

My own love for your continent came first
through her sister-nations:
hearing, seeing, the smoke that thunders;
riding through Zimbabwe's forest with our son
while a herd of zebra cantered by our sides,
keeping pace with our borrowed mounts.
A colony of pied Colobus monkeys chattered among themselves,
Observing us from overhanging trees.
While on the *ile des singes* wise monkeys reigned.

Then there was, for me, the rainbow nation
glorying in newness and in hope.
Where I and colleagues brought the Rowan's fruits
to Grahamstown's cultural explosion
of music, theatre, art and welly boots.

On Robben Island, I walked in the steps
 – the shackled, forgiving steps – of Mandela,
saw the cruel quarry
where he hacked out rocks, and never lost his faith.

At last there was my own embrace of Kenya:
a hard-won courtship and, at last, surrender.
She offered me her children,
her orphaned, abused, neglected children
finding new homes and futures
in Opens Arms' sheltering village.

Month-old Kezia lies sleeping in my arms;
Joseph spoons avocado mash through coal-black lips
into his kitten-pink mouth;
Momma Sereh stoops to her sewing machine.
We sing and dance to God's glory.
At last, I match you in passion for my rival.

PART THREE
SONGS AND BALLADS

THE PLAIN GIRL'S LAMENT

(from the opera Muckle Mou'd Meg)

The road that winds to womanhood
is bleak and bare for the lass that's plain.
There are nae fronds of windblown rose
to pull and keep for calf-love's sake,
for calf-love passes her by.
There are nae meadows of grass and fern
crushed by desire on a simmer's eve.
For the lass that's plain wakes nae desire
and she lies on the grass all alane;
and she daurena dream;
she daurena dream.

The story of the reiver and the lass wi' the muckle mou' (the girl with the big mouth) has been the stuff of ballads and stories for centuries. James Hogg's comic ballad, 'The Fray of Elibank' is probably the most successful of them. I used it as the foundation for the libretto of a short opera for the Scottish Chamber Orchestra. The music was by Chris Achenbach.

BIRDSONG

There were corbie craws in the big ha' lum
    aa stapped wi twigs an' leaves;
there were corps o' doos amang their ain dung,
    an' hoolets in the eaves.

There were nests o' swifts up the turnpike stair
    cemented hard in glaur;
but we made the tower ring wi' steel on stane
    an' the swifts returned nae mair.

The corbie craws fund the lum-heid stapped,
    an' muckle they mourned their loss,
but a wee jenny-wren flitted intae the vault
    and' theeked a nest wi' moss.

There were men aa around, but the wren didnae care:
    she hatched a brood o' fower,
an' she was the last o' the birds o' the air
    made her hame in Aikwood Tower.

During our years at Aikwood, and after I opened the James Hogg exhibition, I welcomed groups of many cultural organisations to the tower. I told them its story through the poetry of the Aikwood cycle. Hilary Bell set some of them to music, and enlivened my talks with her sweet singing.

BRIDE'S SONG

My love built me a bonny bower,
And clad it ower wi' lily flower;
A brawer bower ye ne'er did see
Than my true lover built for me.

The roses scent the evening air,
the western sun lights still my stair,
and through each moment that we wake,
my love and I our pleasure take.

The Ettrick winds beneath my walls,
the first leaf of the autumn falls.
Wi' sic a bield tae keep us warm
we'll fear nae gurly winter storm.

And when the roof is happed wi' snow,
when shimmer white the trees below
by flickering fire and candle-light,
we'll seek the pleasures of the night.

The first verse of this
ballad is taken from
'The Border Widow's
Lament'.

THE BALLAD OF THE THISTLE AND THE LOTUS

For Catriona and Rajiv.

It's high and hot midsummer,
    and the tower bursts into bloom,
not just with old moss-roses,
    with bugle, thrift and broom.
Not just with lady's mantle
    and columbine's many shades
but a bride all gowned in ivory,
    and lapis-blue clad maids;
with gold-encrusted uniforms
    and Rajastani silks,
with embroideries from Kashmir
    and familiar, vivid kilts.

It's high and hot midsummer,
    and there's music in the breeze:
the sounds of pipes and fiddles,
    of sitars and sarangis.
The balladeer's soft singing
    sounds the Ettrick Shepherd's lays,
but her fingers on the clarsach
    pluck a Hindu wedding praise.
There's organ for the kirking,
    Jazz and ceilidh for the feast,
and the tower's old walls reverberate
    to sounds of west and east.

It's high and hot midsummer
　　and the tower springs into life.
In the kirk where she was christened
　　the lass becomes a wife.
Down the village street she walks again
　　where once she walked to school;
where once she played, and rode, and dreamed,
　　she passes, bright and cool.
And the message of all well-wishers,
　　time-honoured as it's brief,
is: joy to pale Catriona,
　　and joy to dark Rajiv!

Was it high and hot midsummer
　　at that marriage long ago,
when Robert Scott of Aikwood
　　took a Murray for his jo?
Did they watch the mason's chisel
　　as their names were cut in stone?
Did they seek an immortality
　　for love that was their own?
Now we send them back a message
　　as new vows are pledged and made:
it's: peace to Elspeth's memory,
　　and peace to Robert's shade!

SONG OF A LONG-AGO RIDE

Tune: the Salley Gardens

For Rory

When I was five-and-twenty,
   and life was trouble-free
I rode with five young horsemen
   in a joyful company.

We rode behind a banner
   where once a king had led,
and from the breasts of my companions
   fluttered ribbons blue and red.

I rode a kind bay gelding
   (Soldier was his name),
and we cantered in the hoofprints
   of an army of great fame.

The wind whipped down the hillside,
   and my horse was blown aside,
but I heard those young men's voices
   raised in chorus on that ride.

Through stormy decades later,
   the memory stayed strong
of the wind that swept the horses,
   and those voices raised in song.

Now I am two-and-sixty,
   the troubled years are fled
and my son rides in those hoofprints
   wearing ribbons blue and red.

TIMBUKTU 72 DAYS

For John Nichol

O, the desert floor's a pitiless path
    of rock and sand and heat,
and our shadows are short in the mid-day glare
    as they mark our camels' feet.
And I think, as the orb of the scorching sun
    beats on each kerchief'd heid:
will I ever again see Yarrow's braes
    or the green haughs of the Tweed?

There are golden pillars that spiral up
    in a frenzied saraband,
and the sun shimmers hot on the rippling waves
    of the limitless sea of sand.
But I dream of the morning mists that rise
    where Yarrow runs quietly down,
and the russet leaves of Ettrick's woods
    that dance to autumn's tune.

For thirty years I ran the Rowan Tree Theatre Company, touring to village halls in the Borders, and to chamber theatre spaces. John Nichol was my close colleague as well as my friend. 1995 saw the bicentenary of the birth of the explorer Mungo Park: he was born in the Yarrow Valley. John wrote a play based on Park's extraordinary feat, I contributed the above song. It was written in pencil on the back of a camel's hump, on a memorable desert trek in Morrocco with my friend Astrid Silins.

51

THE MARCH RIDERS' SONG

Our faces kissed by morning mist, we ride in twaes and threes;
the cherished flag in youth's guid hands streams in the summer breeze.
The rousing notes of flute and pipe are born alang the air,
and Souters drawn frae aa the airts are gathered in the square.
Steady we pass alang the green, steady by hoose and mill,
and crowds at kerb and windae pane rain blessings o' guidwill.
'Safe oot, safe in!' rings in oor heids, and mony a kindly cheer:
    We ride tae keep tradition strong this year and every year!

The Ettrick's flowing broun and swift past pebble, stane and rock;
the current flows round girth and bit, the toun lies at oor back.
Wi' eager mount an' eager hairt we reach the further shore
and stert tae ride the common's mairch o' Selkirk toun yince mair.
The iron hooves' percussion beat sounds up the Linglie Glen
and through the spruce-derk tunnel wi' its fringe o' moss and fern,
till on the hill's hard shoulder, we breathe the heathery air –
    We ride tae keep tradition strong this year and every year!

The shameful side o' Selkirk lies wi' Tibbie Tamson's dust:
the rigid wise, the unco guid, that drove her frae their midst.
Twae hundred simmers later, at her lane grave gie prayer
for the charity and tolerance denied her everywhere.
The triple cairn awaits us on the rooftop of oor warld,
through morning mist, the flag flies free, its ribbons all unfurled.
Noo horses rest, and flasks are passed, and singing fills the air:
    We ride to keep tradition strong this year and every year!

Through burn and bog the horses plunge, their ears pricked hard for home,
and peat flies back frae reckless hooves, and necks are flecked wi' foam.
If you've a canny gelding now, if you've a steady mare
you'll canter on the Peat Law's heights and never gie a care!
The craft flags, bands and followers wait at the Toll in crowds
to spy the burgh's standard in the bield o' Nettly Woods.
O, I'd rather be on horseback now than watching frae afar:
   We ride to keep tradition strong this year and every year!

Alang the narrow bridle path, we're riding knee tae knee,
encircling us, the broad-leaved airch o' mony an ancient tree.
The campion brushes at oor feet, the sycamore at oor hair:
while on the kerb and banking green the welcoming crowd's a-stir.
The Ettrick's crossed, and on the Toll, nae horse needs tae be urged:
on every side a tidal wave o' ringin cheers is heard:
The flag's safe in, and in its wake we race wi'oot a care:
   We ride to keep tradition strong this year and every year!

Steady we pass the hameward streets, steady by shop and hoose,
and here and there tomorrow's riders perch on saddle bows
tae watch the colours cast yince mair in Selkirk's mercat square,
and dream that in some far-off day they'll stand as proudly there.
The Liltin's notes have died away, and noo the flag's returned –
there are tears as weel as cheering, and baith are freely earned,
and each depairting rider in his secret hairt will swear:
   We'll ride to keep tradition strong next year and every year!

THE BALLAD OF AULD NORMAN'S PARTY

In memory of Norman and Maggi Hackett

Part I: *Norman dreams of a party*

It fell about midsummer time,
    when days are lang and fine,
that Norman sat in Languedoc,
    drinking the blood-red wine.

And warmed by France's southern sun,
    he viewed his house with pride:
"My darling Mags, the time has come
    to celebrate!" he cried.

"Next year, when summer suns are high,
    and brightly smiles each morn,
it will be all of three score years
    since you and I were born.

"Because we love the guid red wine,
    still more, a guid malt whisky,
because you smoke your noxious weed,
    and my blood-sugar's risky –

"Because we dine as epicures
    in pleasure and in plenty
we may not reach three score and ten,
    and certainly not twenty.

"So next year, let us celebrate
    ourselves, our friends, our house,
our family and our three score years –
    gird up those loins, my spouse!"

Part 2: *Norman summons his friends.*

Norman has wrocht a braw, braw fax
    aa wi' his ain left hand,
and sent it tae his auldest freends
    that bide in fair Scotland.

He's sent it tae a skeely skipper
    as ever sailed the seas:
his name was Bill, and he did bide
    far, far in cauld Orkney.

He'd landit mony a muckle shark
    and mony a siller haddie,
He feared not wind nor wave nor tide
    this bearded fisher laddie.

But as years passed, the fisher lad
    wi' daith had diced ower often,
for twice the gurly seas had sent
    his ships doun tae the bottom.

Up spak the skipper's loving wife,
    "Auld skills ye must address:
tak up your sketch pad and become
    a limner o' the Press."

As Bill wrocht at his pad yae nicht,
    his fax machine spewed forth
a message frae auld Norman's hoose:
    a summons tae the sooth.

Up spak again the skipper's wife,
    (A pedagogue was she),
"We'll answer Norman's far-flung fax,
    and sail across the sea.

"We'll gang by boat, and car, and train
    until the journey's end,
for Norman since our student years
    has been a foremaist freend."

O, Norman has wrocht anither fax,
    and sealed it wi' his hand,
and sent it tae a smooth courtier
    who dwalt in fair Scotland.

He bided in a bonny hoose
    'neath Edinburgh's castle wa'
and wi' him lived (at each week's end)
    his wife, a justiciar.

Frae Norroway, frae Norroway,
    frae Norroway ower the fame
frae her faither's hoose in Norroway,
    the courtier brocht her hame.

He brocht her first tae Lunnon toun,
    then mony seas and lands,
while he stood aye at the Queen's richt hand
    tae follow her commands.

From time to time, this courtier
    a pen in hand he took,
and aided by a smart pc,
    scrieved mony a weel-wrocht book.

Syne, as the years did onward roll,
    he tired of Lunnon's air,
and tae the Athens o' the north
    yince mair he did repair.

And sae, beneath the castle wa's
    the courtier cooried doun,
and his justiciar wife, at each week's end
    came north frae Lunnon toun.

They read auld Norman's far-flung fax,
    the courtier and his dame:
"We'll tak a flight tae Languedoc
    and then a flight back hame,"

Auld Norman wrocht another fax,
    and, helped by magic power
he sent it tae a Border laird
    dwalt in an auld grey tower.

Tae tell the truth, it was his dame
    dwalt year-long in that peel,
while he gaed sooth tae parliament,
    made mony a weel-judged speil.

The laird gaed sooth tae parliament
    and far-off foreign lands,
exotic isles, and cities far,
    and Afric's golden sands:

While he gaed forth, his patient dame
    bade in the Border tower,
and waited on her lord's return
    through mony a lanesome hour.

Through mony years, tae this same laird
    auld Norman aye had been
a freend baith leal and wondrous dear,
    though seas had rolled atween.

O, mony seas o' guid red wine.
    and o' the guid malt whisky
had douned the thrapples o' this pair
    and made them unco' frisky.

It was as weel that their guid dames
    o' patience were examples,
and aye as weel, o' malt and wine.
    they likewise took odd samples.

And mony a time did Norman send
    unto this laird's guid dame,
a fax of his ain poetry.
    and she sent him the same.

But on this day o' simmer time
    the fax was no' this sort;
'twas a summons to a mighty feast
    o' food, and wine, and malt.

The Border laird he read the fax
    and a loud, loud laugh laughed he:
"I fly sae mony times each year
    we'll get this trip for free."

Auld Norman has wrocht anither fax,
    and sealed it wi' his hand;
he's sent it tae a Baltic quine
    was born in Latvia's land.

This dame she dwalt in elegance
    in Edinboro' and Leith;
by day she plied forceps and drill
    and mended peoples' teeth.

Her spouse, a bearded buirdly chiel,
    frae the Low Countries, I wot:
he wrocht at magic trick wi' lichts –
    a modern Michael Scott.

Like Scott, throughout the far-flung world
    he was a frequent traiveller
and though he lo'ed his Latvian dame,
    lived mainly in Australia.

The Baltic dame, she didnae fear
    tae traivel on her lanesome,
for weel she kenned, in Languedoc,
    she'd find an unco' welcome.

Sae when auld Norman's fax arrived,
    she never did despair,
but bought an Apex ticket that
    by Nice, wad tak' her there.

Part 3:
Norman is struck by a stroke,
but the party happens anyway,

"O, wae is me, o wae is us,"
    wailed Mags, "It's such ill luck:
ayont the wild Atlantic seas,
    my darling Norm's been struck.

*"Auld Norman
aye had been
a freend
baith leal and
wondrous
dear…"*

"On wings provided by Air France
    I'll seek my wounded lover.
meantime, I'm phoning you to say:
    I fear the party's over."

"Not so!" chorused the gallant crew,
    clutching their airline cases,
"We've booked our rooms, and what is more –
    you cannae cancel Apex.

"What though auld Norman wounded lies,
    and Maggi's flown to meet him,
we'll keep a feast, drink deep his health,
    and entertain his children."

It fell about midsummer time,
    when nights are short and starry,
a feast was held, and red wine drunk:
    'twas at La Passifiore.

The toasts were all to absent friends,
    to Norman and his Maggi,
and plans were laid for future feasts
    from Langedoc to Orkney.

And so, despite the blows of fate,
    they partied just the same,
and when the wanderers did return
    freends welcomed them back hame.

Thus ends my lay: a decade's gaun
    since these scenes were enacted.
for food and friendship, wine and malt,
    now let the Lord be thankit.

"He wasnae struck by sword nor spear,
    nor yet by tomahawk,
nor by some mugger lurking near
    in New York's Central Park;

"He wasnae struck by tomahawk,
    nor yet by bow and arrow,
'twas a clot within his cranium
    went coursing through his marrow.

Epilogue

LIFE IS A PERILOUS VOYAGE

With apologies to James Hogg

Take a prospect of human life
from a vista of reason
and you will see
it is a voyage to an undiscovered country.

As we advance
provisions wear out
and the vessel turns crazy.
But the voyage has begun
and we should try to make its conclusion
as happy and prosperous as we can.

What better can we do
than choose true and honest companions?
and with all our skill
steer clear of the quicksands that would swallow us,
steer clear of the rocks that would dash us to pieces.

Thus shall we enter the harbour with hope
and look back on the dangers we've escaped
with pleasure and with exultation.

The Plain Girl's Lament

from Muckle-Mou'd Meg

Prologue (Excerpt)

Libretto: Judy Steel / James Hogg
Music: Chris Achenbach

Birdsong

♩ 120

Lightly

Words: Judy Steel
Music: Hilary Bell

1. There were cor - bie craws – in the big ha' lum
2. There were nests o' swifts – up the turn-pike stair
3. The – cor - bie craws – fand the lum - heid stapped,
4. There were men a' a-roon – but the wren didnae care

– A' stapped – wi' twigs an' leaves;
– Ce - mented – hard - in glaur;
– An' muckle – they mourned their loss;
– She hatched – a brood o' fower;

– There were corps o' doos – a-mang their ain dung -
– But we made the tower – ring wi' steel on stane -
– But a wee jenny wren – flit-ted in tae the vault -
– An' – these were the last – o' the birds o' the air -

– An' hoo – lets - An' hoo – lets -
– An' the swifts – – An' the swifts – –
– An' theeked – – An' theeked – –
– Made their hame – – Made their hame – –

– in the eaves.
– re-turned nae mair.
– a nest wi' moss.
– in Aik - wood Tower. v. 4 Hum

Bride's Song

after

The Border Widow's Lament

Words: Traditional / Judy Steel
Music: Chris Achenbach

Andante semplice

My love built me a bon-ny bow'r And clad it owre — wi — li - ly flow'r; A
ro - ses scent the eve-ning air; The wes-tern sun — lights — still my stair; And

braw - er bow'r ye ne'er did see Than my true lo - ver built for me. The
through each mo - ment that we wake, My love and I our plea - sure

take.

The Ballad of the Thistle and the Lotus

Words: Judy Steel
Music: Hilary Bell

1. It's high and hot mid-sum-mer – and the tow-er bursts in-to

bloom; not just with old moss ro-ses – with bug-le, thrift - and

broom; not just with la-dy's man-tle and col-um-bine's man-y

shades – but a bride - all - gowned in i — vo-ry — And

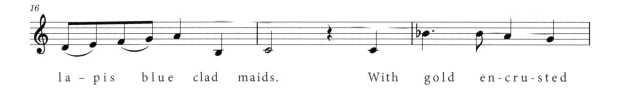

la – pis blue clad maids. With gold en-cru-sted

un-i-forms   and   Ra - ja - sta - ni   silks,   With em-

broi-der-ies   from   Kashmir,   and   fa-mil-i-ar   viv-id   kilts

2. It's high and hot midsummer, and there's music in the breeze:
   the sounds of pipes and fiddles, of sitars and sarangis.
   The balladeer's soft singing sounds the Ettrick Shepherd's lays,
   but her fingers on the clarsach pluck a Hindu wedding praise.
   There's organ for the kirking, Jazz and ceilidh for the feast,
   and the tower's old walls reverberate to sounds of west and east.

3. It's high and hot midsummer and the tower springs into life.
   In the kirk where she was christened the lass becomes a wife.
   Down the village street she walks again where once she walked to school;
   where once she played, and rode, and dreamed, she passes, bright and cool.
   And the message of all well-wishers, time-honoured as it's brief,
   is: joy to pale Catriona, and joy to dark Rajiv!

4. Was it high and hot midsummer at that marriage long ago,
   when Robert Scott of Aikwood took a Murray for his jo?
   Did they watch the mason's chisel as their names were cut in stone?
   Did they seek an immortality for love that was their own?
   Now we send them back a message as new vows are pledged and made:
   it's: peace to Elspeth's memory, and peace to Robert's shade!

Timbuktu 76 Days

Words: Judy Steel
Music: John Nichol / Lucy Cowan

Oh the des-ert floor is a pit-i-less path o' rock and sand and heat- And the sha-dows are short in the noon-day sun as they merk the cam-els' feet- ; And I think, as the orb o' the scorch-in' sun beats- on each ker-chieved heid- , Will I ev-er a-gain see

Yarr - ow's braes, and the green haughs o' the Tweed -

2. There are golden pillars that spiral up in the frenzied saraband,
   And the sun shimmers hot on the rippling waves of the limitless sea of sand.
   But I dream of the morning mists that rise where Yarrow rins quietly doon,
   And the russet leaves of Ettrick's woods that dance tae Autumn's tune.

The March Riders' Song

Words: Judy Steel
Music: Chris Achenbach

Moderately fast

Our __ fa - ces kissed by mor - ning sun, we ride in twaes and threes, The

cher - ished flag in youth's guid hands streams in the sum - mer breeze, The

rou - sing notes of flute and pipe are borne a - lang the air, And

Sou - ters drawn frae a' the airts are ga - thered in the square.

Stea - dy we pass a - lang the Green, stea - dy by hoose and mill, And

crowds at kerb and win - dae - pane rain bles - sings o' guid - will: "Safe

Oot, Safe In!" rings roond our heids, and mo - ny a kind - ly cheer: We

ride to keep trad - i - tion strong this year and e - very year

2. The Ettrick's flowing broun and swift past pebble, stane, and rock;
The current flows roond girth and bit, the toun lies at oor back.
Wi' eager mount and eager hairt we reach the further shore
And stert tae ride the common's mairch o' Selkirk toun yince mair
The iron hooves' percussion beat sounds up the Linglie Glen
And through the spruce-derk tunnel wi' its fringe o' moss and fern,
Till on the hill's hard shoulder, we breathe the heathery air -
We ride to keep tradition strong this year and every year.

3. The shameful side o' Selkirk lies wi' Tibbie Tamson's dust:
The rigid wise, the unco guid, that drave her frae their midst.
Twae hundred simmers later, at her lane grave gie prayer
For the charity and tolerance denied her everywhere.
The triple cairn awaits us on the rooftop of oor warld,
Through morning mist, the flag flies free, its ribbons all unfurled.
Noo horses rest, and flaks are passed, and singing fills the air:
We ride to keep tradition strong this year and every year.

4. Through burn and bog the horses plunge, their ears pricked hard for hame,
And peat flies back frae reckless hooves, and necks are flecked wi' foam.
If you've a canny gelding now, if you've a steady mare
You'll canter on the Peat Law's heights and never gie a care!
The craft flags, bands and followers wait at the Toll in crowds
To spy the burgh's standard in the bield o' Nettly woods.
O, I'd rather be on horseback now than watching frae afar:
We ride to keep tradition strong this year and every year.

5. Alang the narrow bridle path, we're riding knee tae knee,
Encircling us, the braid-leaved arch o' mony an ancient tree.
The campion brushes at oor feet, the sycamore at oor hair:
On pavement and on banking green the welcoming crowd's astir.
The Ettrick's crossed, and on the Toll, nae horse needs tae be urged:
On ilka side a tidal wave o' ringing cheers is heard:
The flag's safe in, and in its wake we race wi'oot a care:
We ride to keep tradition strong this year and every year.

6. Steady we pass the hameward streets, steady by shop and hoose,
And here and there tomorrow's riders perch on saddle bows
Tae watch the colours cast yince mair in Selkirk's mercat square,
And dream that in some far-off day they'll stand as proudly there.
The Liltin's notes have died away, and noo the flag's returned:
There are tears as weel as cheering, and baith are freely earned;
And each departing rider in his secret hairt will swear:
We ride to keep tradition strong this year and every year.

67

GLOSSARY

A

aa	all
aik	oak
airts	directions
an	and
atween	between
auld	old
auld-Farrant	old-fashioned

B

bield	shelter
birkie	young man
blaw	blow
braid	broad
braw	handsome, beautiful
buirdly	well-built
bunnet	bonnet
bussing	decorating a flag by tying ribbons on to it

C

callant	young man
carlin	old woman
chiel	man
coorie	snuggle
corbie craw	crow

D

derk	dark
dizzen	dozen
dyke	wall

F

fiere	close friend
fit	foot
forrit	forward

G

garron	Highland pony
gowd	gold
guid	good
gurly	stormy

H

hairt	heart
happed	wrapped
haugh	area of flat ground, usually beside a river
haund	hand
heid	head
hempen	made of hemp
hunnert	hundred

I

ilka	every

J

jaiket	jacket
jo	sweetheart

K

kerry-handed	left handed

L

leal	loyal
lift	sky
the Liltin	the words by Jean Elliot to the lament *The Flowers o' the Forest*
lowering *(soft ow, cf how)*	brooding, moody
lum	chimney

M

march, mairch	boundary
muckle	much, big

N

nicht afore	night before *(usually a celebration)*

O

ower, owre	over

P

peel	a border tower
pealie-wallie	feeble
plaidie	plaid (garment)
preen	show off

R

rade	rode
reiver	Border thief, mainly 15-16th century

S

sax	six
seevin	seven
schule	school
siller	silver
skeelly	skilful
souter	native of Selkirk
speil	speech
streekit	stretched
swire	the watershed between two valleys

T

theeked	thatched, wove
Teri	native of Hawick
thon	that
toun	town
thrapple	throat
troosers	trousers
tumshie	turnip
twae	two

U, W

unco guid	hypocritical
windae	window
wrocht	made skilfully

Y

yae, yin	one